101 Celtic crosses

courtney davis

David & Charles

A DAVID & CHARLES BOOK

First published in 2004

Distributed in North America
by F&W Publications, Inc.
4700 East Galbraith Road
Cincinnati, OH 45236
1-800-289-0963

A catalogue record for this book is available from the British Library.

ISBN 0 7153 1667 2 paperback

Printed in Singapore by KHL Printing Co Pte Ltd
for David & Charles
Brunel House Newton Abbot Devon

Commissioning Editor Neil Baber
Desk Editor Sandra Pruski
Designer Nigel Morgan
Production Controller Kelly Smith

I dedicate this book to my daughter Bridie, may her light always shine.

My grateful thanks to Father Dennis O'Neill and the staff at David & Charles for their input on this book.

Visit our website at www.davidandcharles.co.uk

David & Charles books are available from all good bookshops; alternatively you can contact our Orderline on (0)1626 334555 or write to us at FREEPOST EX2110, David & Charles Direct, Newton Abbot, TQ12 4ZZ (no stamp required UK mainland).

101 Celtic crosses

contents

introduction by dennis o'neill

Among the ancient artifacts in the National Museum of Ireland there is a sheet-gold crescent-shaped ornament, partially framing a gold solar disc, upon which is engraved an equal-armed cross. Apparently incised with the universal sign of Christianity, this disc could easily be a Communion plate. In fact it is a 4000-year-old votive offering to Áine, one of the oldest of the chief pre-Christian deities worshipped in Ireland's southern province of Munster. When the Celts first arrived in Ireland the cult of their mother goddess Anu (after whom the Danube and several other rivers are named) was absorbed into that of Áine, demonstrating a typical Celtic pattern of cultural assimilation. St Patrick's appreciation of the spiritual value of much of Celtic learning and culture led him to 'baptize' as much of it as he deemed compatible with Christianity. When he proclaimed the cross as the quintessential symbol of Christianity, he was teaching the Celts to recognize a new level of meaning in a symbol they already revered.

The Symbol of the Cross

The use of the cross as a Christian symbol is traceable back to the time of the Roman persecution. In Rome itself is the earliest known undisputed depiction of a cross in a Christian context. Dated to around 220, it is a mocking graffito incised onto the wall of the Roman army cadets' garrison on the Palatine Hill. It shows a crucified man with the head of an ass, and next to it a young man standing in reverence. The accompanying Greek text says *Alexamenos worships his God*. This is a clear indication that early Christians publicly proclaimed the cross as the central symbol of their faith, even before the time it was adopted as such by Constantine, the first Christian Emperor.

A frequently used ancient Christian symbol for the cross was a monogram made by combining the two Greek letters *X (chi)* and *P (rho)*, the first and second letters of the word Christ. This sign can be found inscribed on the walls of the catacombs in Rome and other places where Christians gathered. Along with the Latin message *In hoc signo vinces* (in this sign, conquer), the *Chi-Rho* monogram appeared to Constantine in a vision. As a result he displayed the symbol on the standards that flew before his army at the great victory against Maxentius, his rival for Emperor, at Milvian Bridge in 312. Because Constantine attributed the victory to Christ, the following year he put an end to the persecution of Christians within the Empire. From then on, the cross quickly surpassed the *Chi-Rho* and every other symbol as the pre-eminent emblem of Christianity.

By the following century, when St Patrick was evangelizing in Ireland, he blessed everyone and everything with the sign of the cross. Both of his 7th-century biographers mention the erection of crosses in connection with his mission. Muirchú's *Life of St Patrick* refers to a cross, still extant in Muirchú's day, which marked the place in Slemish, Co. Antrim, where Patrick had been a slave and later returned to meet his former master, Miliuc. Bishop Tirechán's *Account of St Patrick's Journey* mentions that the saint 'erected a stone marked with the cross of Christ' in Bartragh, Co. Sligo. A 7th-century life of St Samson in Cornwall describes the way the bishop found pagans dancing around a stone and how, after converting them, he marked the sacred stones with crosses. An example of a similarly inscribed stone is a boulder at Kilcolman, on Ireland's Dingle Peninsula, marked with two Maltese crosses (four arms of equal length, each arm ending in a cleft or two short pointed branches), one of which lies in a circle, and an inscription in Ogham – the ancient Druidic script.

Earliest Examples

The pillar stone in Llangernwy, north Wales, has nothing more than a small cross carved on it, which means that it was probably originally a pre-Christian *menhir*, or standing stone. Many of these ancient standing stones were similarly 'Christianized' throughout the Celtic lands. They seem to have served originally as a sort of *axis mundi* (axis of the world), a vertical totem frequently placed in the centre of a village as a connector between worlds. In many places in south Wales, the earliest freestanding crosses, dating from the 5th century, were composed of carved cross heads attached to more ancient shafts.

Many memorial gravestones incised with the *Chi-Rho* monogram were erected from the 4th to the 8th centuries, particularly in Munster. On a mountain in Arraglen, Co. Kerry, stands a pillar bearing on one side a Greek cross (with vertical and horizontal bars of the same length) incised in a circle; on the other side is a *Chi-Rho* monogram with an inscription in Ogham. In a wall near the ruins of St Non's chapel at St David's in Wales is an ancient stone inscribed with a simple Latin cross (an upright bar crossed near the top by a shorter transverse). This cross is imposed on a disc, representing the face of the sun. Sometimes crosses were simply carved in the rock – as on the rock outside St Ninian's cave at Whithorn in Galloway, Scotland. There are slabs and pillars with monograms of Greek, Latin or Maltese crosses throughout Ireland, often decorated with some early curvilinear forms, including knots, swastikas and sunbursts.

Swastikas are ancient pre-Christian symbols for the sun. Elaborate swastikas can be seen in the two discs at the feet of the Saviour on the Portrait of Christ page of the Book of Kells; and a fine example of a sunburst cross is carved on a stele, or pillar, in a churchyard at Carndonagh, Co. Donegal. There are also two pilgrim figures carved on either side of it, in an attitude of veneration. What actually may be represented is a *flabellum*, a liturgical fan often used by deacons in the liturgical practice of the East, but rarely in the West. Their appearance in a Celtic carving clearly points to Byzantine influence. St Columba owned one, recorded to have survived as a relic on Iona until 1034, when it was lost at sea. Whereas Eastern *flabella* could be made of many things, from peacock feathers to metal discs, upon which were incised the burning face of seraphs, the Celts seem to have favoured a solar disc design. Three solar-design *flabella* are shown in the hands of the angels venerating the Virgin and Child in the Book of Kells. It is also interesting that the angel painted to represent St Matthew on the Evangelists page of the Book of Kells is holding a processional cross identical to the *flabella* elsewhere in the book, except that here the *flabellum* serves as the central portion of a Greek cross.

There are many examples of early crucifixes among the stone crosses. At Kilnasaggart, Co. Armagh, there is a stone carved with an early crude relief of a crucified Christ, attended by the centurion, who is holding up to his lips a spear, on the point of which is a sponge. On full cruciform slabs on Inishkea Island, Co. Mayo, and at Carndonagh, Co. Donegal, there are incised Crucifixions and other figures. In many ages and places, stones have been venerated for their supposed powers and virtues. Such stones, especially in Brittany, have been Christianized, in the sense that they have been either marked or surmounted with a later cross.

The Northumbrian king St Oswald is recorded as having set up a wooden cross on the isle of Iona in 635. By the time St Adomnán (died 704) was abbot, several others had been erected. The earliest inscribed monuments along

Scotland's west coast are grave-slabs from Iona. The fine early crosses of St Oran, St John, and St Martin, also on Iona, all show signs of derivation from timber prototypes. Closely related in style to the St Martin's cross is the Kildalton cross on Islay, a fine product of the Iona school. The earliest freestanding stone crosses on the west coast are at Ruthwell and Bewcastle, both of them 7th century Northumbrian. None of the stone crosses in Cornwall dates from earlier than the 6th or 7th century.

High Crosses

Dating from the 8th century onward, the great freestanding high crosses of Ireland, remain some of the most striking monuments of Celtic Christianity. Despite the destruction of the Reformation, there are still many stone crosses in north and west Britain. About a hundred remain in Ireland and 270 in Cornwall alone. Most are of granite and have been fashioned with iron tools. Many are carved from high quality dressed stone, standing on foursquare pyramidal bases, which represent the world-mountain whose roots are deep in the earth. Crowning the upright shaft is a Celtic cross with a sun-wheel circling the crossing – the unique and distinctive characteristic of the Celtic cross.

Some of the finest high crosses – such as those at Clonmacnois, Killamery and Monasterboice – are topped with house-like shingle-roofed capstones, symbolizing the heavenly abode. These crosses are covered with carvings of elaborate Celtic designs or scenes from the scriptures. The base of the beautifully decorated 8th-century North Cross at Ahenny has a carved bas-relief of a funeral procession, led by a monk carrying a Celtic cross – possibly an indication that some of the stone crosses were modelled on earlier wooden or metal processional crosses.

Another series of high crosses appeared in Ireland during the 12th century, though solar discs were less prevalent than in earlier times. This is due to the influence of the Normans, who came into the country in the latter half of the 12th century and began to introduce larger churches and less dramatic crosses. The ringed Celtic cross did not reappear until the national and political resurgence of a sense of Celtic identity took place in Ireland during the 19th century.

Decorative Embellishment

Until the advent of Christianity, Celtic was also an almost entirely oral tradition. Skilled bards would memorize texts and then verbally embellish them to mesmerize an audience while teaching and entertaining them. But Christianity was a religion of the Book: it required bibles, psalters, gospels and prayer books. With their background of the old Druidic tradition, the earliest monks and nuns not only produced the needed sacred books but embellished them with colours and designs which provided the visual equivalent of bardic oral embellishment.

This led to supreme artistic excellence in book illuminating, but also in metal- and enamel-work, filigree-working, and stone carving. Many of the sacred designs on stone crosses of this period can be seen with much more intricate detail on contemporary samples of metallurgy – the shrines, reliquaries, book covers, pectoral and processional crosses and so on that have survived from the Middle Ages. One example is a splendid jeweled Greek cross in a circle on a late 7th century masterpiece, the Ardagh chalice. Another is St Cuthbert's golden pectoral cross set with red garnets, which was buried with him on Lindisfarne island in 687. Lindisfarne and its mother house on Iona both trace their origins to St Columba and are the principal foundations where the eclectic 8th-century art styles of Northumbria and Ireland came to full fruition.

The first major monument to this new style is the Book of Durrow. Made late in the 7th century, it is the earliest surviving elaborately ornamented Celtic manuscript. It contains a page showing a Latin cross, embellished with intricate knotwork, with stylized images representing the four evangelists in the corners *(see chapter 3 title page)*. Many of the illuminated gospel books which came after the Book of Durrow have carpet pages providing colourful settings for splendidly designed crosses. The late 7th-century St Chad Gospel has a page with a Latin cross filled with intricate knotted bird designs on a carpet surface covered with a plethora of zoomorphic interlaced swastikas, in which portions of other animals are knotted together. The splendid Lindisfarne Gospels were completed during the same period and include carpet pages, one of which shows a Latin cross filled and surrounded with triskelions (swirling designs with three spirals radiating from a common centre).

Among the most glorious examples of Celtic monastic metalwork which have survived to the present are sacred items which were fashioned in the century before the Norman invasion of Ireland. Some of them were shrines for the most revered sacred books. The Shrine of the Cathach was created at Kells late in the 11th century. The front side is covered with jewels and with bas-reliefs showing St Columba, an enthroned youthful Christ, and a Crucifixion scene. The back of the shrine bears an openwork design of pierced Greek crosses. The front of the 12th-century shrine of the Book of Dimma is also encrusted with jewels and quartered by a large Greek cross, in which there is the relief of smaller Latin cross. The other panels alternate incised cross and knotwork designs. On the front panel of the 12th-century shrine for the relics of St Manchan is a beautiful Greek cross with round bosses at its centre and four terminals, all of which are incised with intricate knotwork patterns quartered by smaller Greek crosses. The shrine which contained St Patrick's bell also dates from this period and has on its front a lovely cross, paneled with spiral and knotwork designs and encrusted with jewels.

A New Era

If the 12th-century Norman invasion of Ireland dealt a blow to the uniquely Celtic flavour of sacred design, the 16th-century Reformation destroyed most of its surviving examples. However, the resurgence of Irish nationalism that culminated in the establishment of the Irish Republic in 1922 coincided with resurgent appreciation of Celtic music, literature and art. The Celtic cross began to appear everywhere again as a symbol of freedom, faith, and national spirit. While the Catholic Church had a lot of influence during this period and certainly encouraged use of the Celtic cross as a symbol of the ancient faith, Protestant churches also valued and used it as the symbol which most powerfully expressed their special blend of national and Christian identity.

Now, in the 21st century, as the power of more organized and hierarchical Christianity shows signs of waning, many people have sought to return to the values of the ancient Celtic church: its style of governance and use of authority in a way more suited to the needs and the experience of the people, its unusually high esteem for women, artists, and musicians, its respect for pre-Christian culture and faith and its ecological sensitivity. Many who wear a Celtic cross these days do so both as an expression of faith and of the embracing of these values. After all, the Celtic cross not only combines the symbol of Christ with the disc of the sun but it also represents the *axis mundi* – the hypothetical line in reference to which everyone and everything is in harmony and symmetry.

designs in stone

designs in stone

This tombstone of a smith is one of a fine collection of more than 500 fragments or complete monuments carved with Celtic crosses, names and invocations in ancient script.
Clonmacnois, Co. Offaly, Ireland

Recumbent cross slabs were the forerunners of headstones and were more common in Ireland than elsewhere in the British Isles. This simple knotwork cross on an Irish tomb slab is dated around 800. *Clonmacnois, Co. Offaly, Ireland*

three

designs in stone

A restored cross slab featuring a key pattern and knotwork design.
Fuerty, Co. Roscommon, Ireland

The swastika was originally a pagan symbol for lightning and is found on early Greek coins and pottery, as well as the feet of some Buddhas. Although adopted by early Christians and found on three sepulchre slabs in Ireland, it was never a common Christian symbol.

designs in stone

Incised design on a stone cross slab. *Ballyvourney, Co. Cork, Ireland*

Many examples of this carved stone cross can be found in Scotland and Ireland. The knotwork arms of the cross form into triquetras, symbolizing the Holy Trinity.

A 9th-century cross slab with key pattern design in the form of a cross. *St David's Cathedral, Pembrokeshire, Wales*

Cross design taken from the carved reverse side of a cross slab from Ulbster. The design is made up of triangular knotwork and is without end. *Ulbster, Caithness, Scotland*

Design from an 8th-century cross slab at Clonmacnois. The outer key pattern border is similar to that found on a cross shaft at St Andrew's in Scotland. *Clonmacnois, Co. Offaly, Ireland*

Part of the Abraham Stone, a grave marker now embedded in an interior wall. This fine example of 11th-century Celtic art has a Christian cross interwoven with Celtic knotwork and inscriptions. *St David's Cathedral, St David's, Pembrokeshire, Wales*

eleven

designs in stone

Section from the Inchbrayock Stone, showing the ringed cross carved with stepped armpits, a spiral pattern in the arms, and key pattern in the centre. *Montrose Museum, Montrose, Scotland*

designs in stone

Top section of the Aberlemno cross slab. *Aberlemno churchyard, Angus, Scotland*

thirteen

Cross pillar with face decorated with a hexafoil design which was probably set out with a compass. Geometrical patterns fashioned with the use of a compass were not unusual in the 7th century. *Carndonagh, Co. Donegal, Ireland*

Adaptation of the ornamented Rosemarkie cross, carved in red sandstone. The existing fragment standing over 2.7m (8ft) high was carved around the 8th century. *Groam House Museum, Rosemarkie, Ross-shire, Scotland*

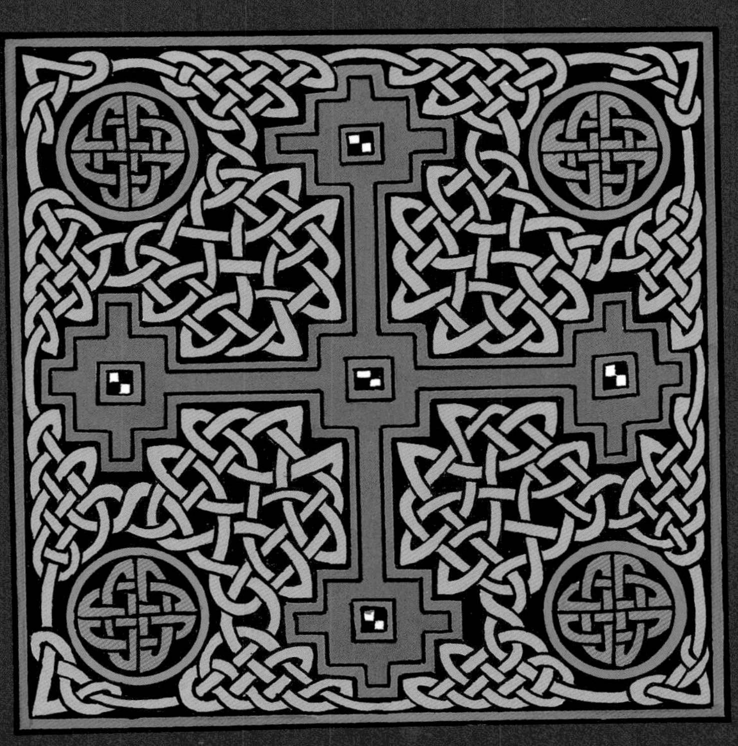

The 8th-century Fahan cross slab is filled with a simple knotwork cross. *Fahan Mura, Co. Donegal, Ireland*

An early 8th-century cross slab at Gallen Priory illustrates the story of Jonah and the whale in low relief with a snake boss spiral at the centre. *Gallen, Co. Offaly, Ireland*

seventeen

Slab cross from Kirk Conchan is decorated with an interlaced design with the guardian dogs of Conchem (St Christopher) at the base. The stone dates from around the late 8th century. *Kirk Conchan, Isle of Man*

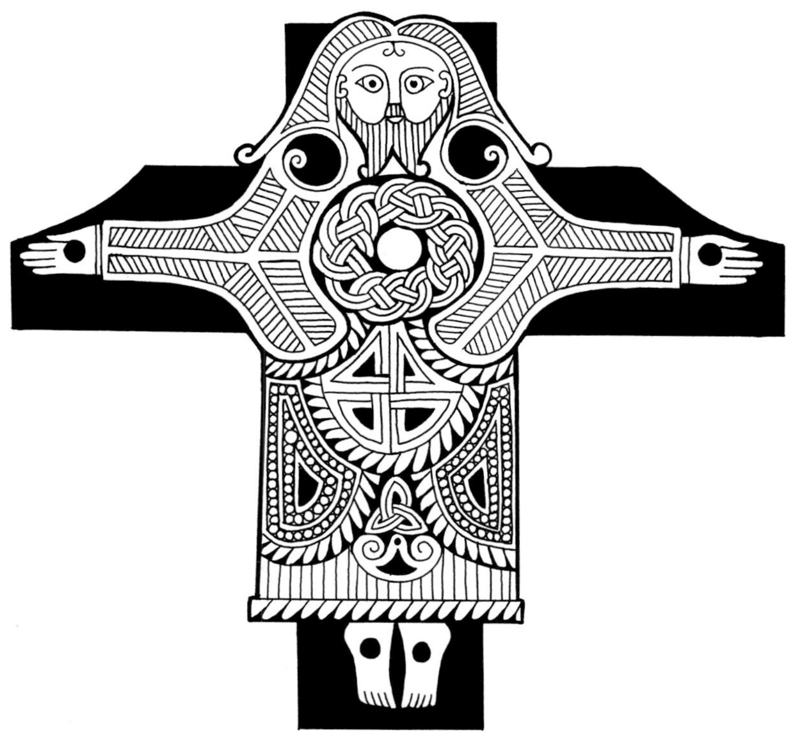

The 8th-century Calf of Man Crucifixion slab was perhaps copied from a bronze plaque that adorned a book cover. Only half of the slab remains intact and the picture above is an interpretation of the complete image. *Manx Museum, Douglas, Isle of Man*

nineteen

An adaptation of an 8th-century wickerwork cross from Kirk Conchan. The stone is carved to follow the outline of the wheelhead and is one of the forerunners of the later freestanding stone crosses. *Kirk Conchan, Isle of Man*

Fragment of an 8th-century cross design from a cross slab at Clonmacnois. The outer step pattern border is similar to the classical Greek fret. *Clonmacnois, Co. Offaly, Ireland*

The most distinctive form of cross slab elaboration in South Wales was the development of the ring cross. The illustration is taken from the late 9th-century Houelt slab cross. *Margam, Glamorgan, Wales*

Detail from the 8th-century Hilton of Cadboll stone with two threads of knotwork forming a simple cross pattern. *Royal Museum of Scotland, Edinburgh*

Design adapted from a panel on the Ulbster Stone. *Ulbster, Caithness, Scotland*

Knotwork cross design from an 8th-century stone slab at Clonmacnois, renowned for its fine collection of Celtic carvings. *Clonmacnois, Co. Offaly, Ireland*

Knotwork panel from the Glamis stone. *Glamis, Angus, Scotland*

The 8th-century Tullylease cross, with its labyrinth of key patterns, is considered to be the finest early Christian cross slab in Ireland. *St Berichter Monastery, Co. Cork, Ireland*

The 9th-century St Fergus Manse cross slab stone. *Glamis, Angus, Scotland*

The early 8th-century Aberlemno cross slab has Northumbrian animals on the front and Pictish symbols on the back, possibly representing the battle of Nechtansmere fought nearby in 685. *Aberlemno churchyard, Angus, Scotland*

twenty-nine

The east face of the 9th-century Celtic high cross at Killamery has four entwined serpents. The serpent is believed to have been the Celtic symbol of healing and this carving may represent resurrection and rebirth. *Killamery, Co. Kilkenny, Ireland*

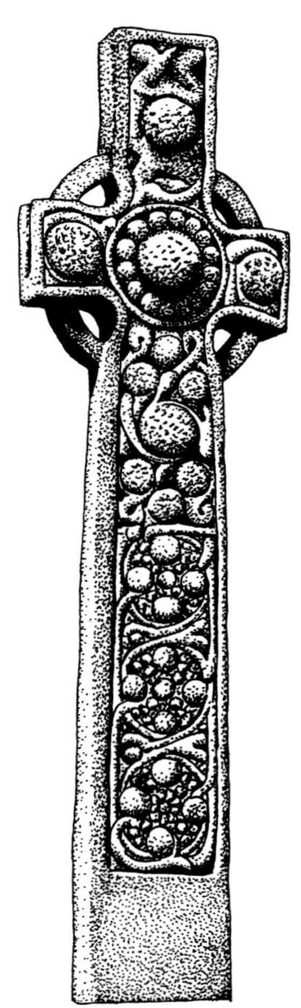

Carved in the late 8th century the St Martin's cross is a fine example of the 'boss style' of decoration – a convex half round shape decorated in knotwork. The arms of the cross have slots possibly for wooden or metal extensions used to hold ribbons or garlands.
Iona, Scotland

Carvings of bishops carrying three different types of crosiers adorn the 12th-century Doorty cross. *Kilfenora, Co. Clare, Ireland*

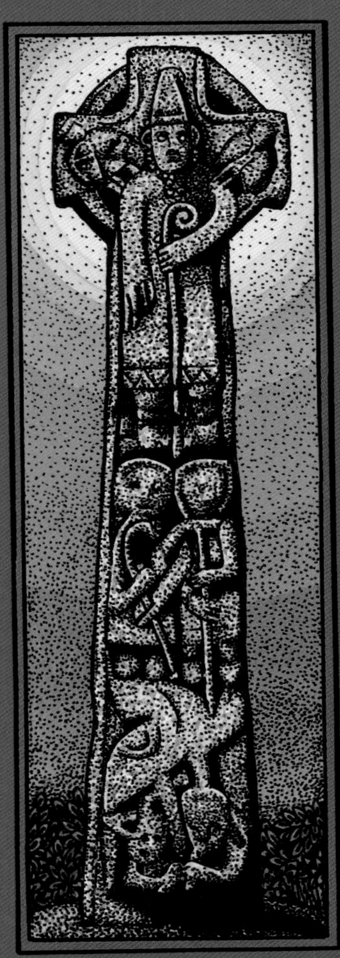

The head of the 10th-century Nevern cross is much smaller in diameter in proportion to its height of 4m (12ft); it was constructed separately and then fixed to the shaft by means of a mortise and tenon. *Nevern churchyard, Dyfed, Wales*

The early 10th-century Neuadd Siarman cross is considered to be one of the finest carved stones in Wales. *Brecknock Museum, Powys, Wales*

The reverse side of the Neuadd Siarman cross.
Brecknock Museum, Powys, Wales

Based on a 9th-century Irish cross slab. *Carndonagh, Co. Donegal, Ireland*

A 15th-century West Highland cross. *Kildalton, Islay, Scotland*

The 19th-century gravestone cross of the Welsh bard Tegid, co-translator of the series of eleven Celtic tales from The Mabinogian. *St Brynach's, Nevern, Dyfed, Wales*

thirty-eight

Part of the 19th-century high cross for Ellen and William Burke in Glasnevin cemetery.
Glasnevin cemetery, Dublin

Early 20th-century gravestone of Cecil Bendall, Professor of Sanskrit at Cambridge University. *St Giles cemetery, Cambridge, England*

Some high crosses, like those at Monasterboice (on which this is based), were thought to act as preaching points rather than being solely commemorative. *Monasterboice, Co. Louth, Ireland*

Design adapted from the 8th-century Fahan cross slab. *Fahan, Co. Donegal, Ireland*

Based on a 19th-century carving over the west door of a church in Rathdaire.
Church of Ireland, Rathdaire, Co. Laois, Ireland

designs in metalwork

From a medallion inlaid with glass and enamel studs on the 8th-century Ardagh chalice discovered in 1980 in Co. Tipperary and probably made either in Ireland or Northumbria. *National Museum of Ireland, Dublin*

Silver and enamel panel from the Moylough belt shrine made to preserve a leather girdle that is still contained within it. The panel is surrounded by L-shaped cloisons filled with enamel. *National Museum of Ireland, Dublin*

The 12th-century Lismore Crosier is recognized as one of the finest example of ornamental metalwork, combining Irish and Viking ornament. *National Museum of Ireland, Dublin*

forty-six

A copper alloy and enamel hanging bowl mount, dating from the 6th or 7th century and decorated with a pair of dolphins with open mouths. The bodies loop under themselves to form a blunt tail against the cross arms. *Faversham, Kent, England*

forty-seven

Design from a copper alloy and enamel hanging bowl mount. The Latin cross with slightly expanded arms sits upon a four lobed knot, with triquetras in each corner. *Whitby Abbey, Yorkshire, England*

Forty-eight

Detail from a cast copper harness mount found in Ireland and dated between the 8th and 9th centuries. *Navan, Co. Meath, Ireland*

This 11th-century silver crucifix from a hoard found in Sweden shows Christ bound to a cross rather than nailed. *Statens Historiska Museum, Stockholm, Sweden*

fifty

Irish enamelled and gilded copper-alloy mount dated to the 8th or 9th century.
Universitetets Oldsaksamling, Oslo, Norway

St Cuthbert's cross is a descendent of earlier 7th century garnet inlaid pectoral crosses. Made in Northumberland it may have been worn by St Cuthbert before his death in 687.
St Cuthbert's tomb, Durham Cathedral, England

designs in illuminated manuscripts

A small cross within the main illuminated page of St Mark's Gospel in the Book of Kells. *Trinity College, Dublin*

The roundel design containing a curved, splayed, equal-armed cross, against a step patterned background is taken from the centre of a cross-carpet page of the 7th-century Book of Durrow. *Trinity College, Dublin*

The slim and straight-sided cross from the four Evangelists' symbols page in the Book of Durrow. It is filled with a knotwork pattern which swells out into short, broad, basin-shaped extensions at the ends of the arms and stem. *Trinity College, Dublin*

Knotwork cross panel taken from a decorated border surrounding the portrait of St John in the Book of Kells. *Trinity College, Dublin*

Entwined serpents, from a section of The Temptation of Christ in the Book of Kells.
Trinity College, Dublin

A cross design from the beginning of St John's Gospel in the 9th-century Book of Kells.
Trinity College, Dublin

Entwined serpents adapted from a section of The Temptation of Christ in the Book of Kells. The snake often represented Christ's resurrection, from the belief that it renewed its youth when it shed its skin. *Trinity College, Dublin*

fifty-nine

The step pattern is part of a cross-carpet page introducing St Jerome's letter to the Pope in the Lindisfarne Gospels. *British Library, London*

A carpet page from the early 8th-century Echternach Gospels containing a cross filled with diagonal key patterns. *Universitatsbibliothek, Augsburg, Germany*

sixty-one

Section of a cross-carpet page from the 7th-century Book of Durrow, the earliest surviving fully illuminated Gospel from the British Isles. Probably from a monastic foundation of St Columba in Ireland, Northumbria or Iona. *Trinity College, Dublin*

sixty-two

A fine knotwork cross design from the opening decorated page of the *Collectio canonum* MS213. The script and style of decoration indicates that it was probably created in Northumbria in the 8th century. *Dombibliothek, Cologne, Germany*

Design from the stencilled decoration of an Oratory at the Dominican Convent at Dunlaoghaire by Sister Concepta Lynch. *Dominican Convent, Dunlaoghaire, Co. Dublin, Ireland*

Based on knotwork designs in the Book of Kells.

Cross of the Four Directions, based on an illuminated panel in the Canterbury Bible.
British Library, London

Durrow cross, adapted from a section of a carpet page in the Book of Durrow.
Trinity College, Dublin, Ireland

modern
designs

Cross of the Spirit – the arms of this simple knot cross are each filled with the three armed peltas which symbolize the Holy Trinity.

In Celtic symbolism the circle represents wholeness, the round contours of the Earth, or female energy, and the cross represents the four directions of movement, or male energy, in the form of winds, seasons and so forth.

The spiral triskele patterns placed between the arms were a well-known symbol for the sun during the Bronze Age (2500-700BC).

Cross of St Ita – knotwork symbolizes the continuity of existence and the main vocation of the 6th-century saint was to teach her pupils the concept of the saints, whether alive or dead, being seen as 'soul friends', to be confidantes and confessors.

The Cross of the Holy Spirit – the tongues of fire are a symbol of the power of the Holy Spirit, described in The Acts of The Apostles.

Cross of Thorns – like the Tree of Life, the cross stands for the 'world-axis'. Placed in the mystic centre of the cosmos, it becomes a bridge by which the soul may reach God.

Fiery Cross of Inspiration – passing through fire is thought to be symbolic of transformation and regeneration to transcend the human condition.

St Brigid's Cross – tradition says that while the saint was tending a dying pagan, she spent her time in prayer and plaited some rushes into the shape of an equal-armed cross. It is still hung over many Irish doorways as a protection for the home.

In memory of their founder, the nuns of the convent of St Brigid of Kildare always kept a fire burning. Surrounding the cross is an oak wreath representing Kildare and symbolizing faith and endurance.

Cross of the Spirit – the signs for infinity here are at once interlacing and knotted, emphasizing the relation of the knot to the idea of infinity. The Celts firmly believed in the continuation of existence from this world to the next and beyond.

Cross of St Bridget – born around 453, the saint's feast is celebrated on 1 February, which coincides with the pagan Celtic fire festival of Imbolc, marking the return of the light after the darkness of winter. In Christian symbolism the dogs at the base of the cross have the function of a sheepdog, guarding the flock, so they may also become an allegory for the priest.

Cross of Light – the spiral triskele at the heart of the cross is a very ancient symbol for the sun, symbolizing the still centre, the meeting place of heaven and earth.

St Patrick's High Cross – in his mission to bring Christianity to the Irish, St Patrick incorporated much of the spirituality of the pre-Christian Celtic tradition. Even the Celtic cross evolved from the ancient symbol of the divine sunwheel.

A simple Celtic knot cross designed to express harmony and balance.

eighty-one

Solar Cross – inspired by the goddess Brigid who had a solar, as well as lunar, aspect. One of her many names was Breo-saigit or 'fiery arrow', identifying her with the first ray of sunshine of the Winter Solstice. A Celtic goddess adopted by the Christians, perhaps?

Interlaced cross – in the middle of the 7th century the first interlacing appears in insular book decoration in a fragment of the Durham Gospels. The ability of knotwork to expand or contract to fill a designated space made it a useful decorative tool for Celtic scribes.

Cross of Inner Peace – the basic symbolism of Celtic knotwork design is that of the 'great cosmic loom of the universe'. The unbroken interwoven band symbolizes the continuity of the spirit.

It is believed that some of the highly decorated crosses were used by the early Celtic church as preaching points rather than being purely commemorative. The decoration would have been painted to visually display the glory of God to the congregation.

Easter Cross – recalling Christ's Passion, the thorns represent the idea of existence and non-existence, ecstasy and anguish.

This style is used by some modern Celtic artists to represent the Isle of Iona, which in Gaelic means the Isle of Saints. St Columba landed there in 563 with twelve companions and founded the monastery where, it is believed, the Book of Kells was begun.

The ability of the knotwork to expand or contract, like liquid filling every available space, made it a useful decorative tool for the Celtic scribe.

Cross of St Hilda – the coiled serpents refer to the legend of her prayers changing dangerous snakes into stones.

To the early Celtic Christians the Celtic cross is a symbolic spiritual diagram, sometimes called a mandala. The four 'directions' of the cross or male energy are surrounded by the roundness of female energy in harmonious balance.

Cross of St Cuthbert – inspired by decoration in the 8th-century Lindisfarne Gospels in honour of St Cuthbert.

Knotwork carpet cross – the basic symbolism of Celtic knotwork design (an unbroken interwoven band) is thought by many to be the idea of eternity.

Triskele cross – the triskele was an ancient Celtic symbol which adorned the most sacred places. Representing the trinity of life, it also represents the Goddess in all her forms – maiden, mother, and crone.

Cross of Contemplation – the four arms of the cross represent the four seasons, the cyclic changes of nature as it moves through each season and the constancy of the cycle of life, death and rebirth echoed in pre-Christian as well as Christian festivals.

Cross of Reflection – incorporating the distinctive woven knotwork design symbolic of eternity.

Cross of Reflection II – an adaptation of the cross on the previous page, formed by splitting the knotwork ribbon in two.

Inspired by designs found within the Lindisfarne Gospels, the cross is a tribute to St Aidan, the 7th-century monk of Iona who was invited by the Christian King Oswald to evangelize the northern parts of England and was later consecrated Bishop of Lindisfarne.

Knotwork cross incorporating the distinctive Celtic sunwheel imposed on the arms of the cross.

The unbroken strand of knotwork is a recurrent theme in Celtic decoration, symbolizing the continuity of existence.

The first appearance of interlacing is on the colophon page at the end of St Matthew's Gospel from a fragment of the 7th-century Durham Gospels.

Many high crosses are decorated with a house cap, representing a Celtic oratory or shrine in miniature.

Emerald Cross – in Christian symbolism green is associated with spring, the triumph of life over death and the regeneration of the soul through good works.

Source Material

The Romano British Period and Celtic Monuments
J Romilly Allen, Llanerch Publishers 1992

The Celtic Cross
Nigel Pennick, Blandford Press,1997

Celtic Crosses of Britain and Ireland
Malcom Seaborne, Shire Publications, 1989

Art of the Celts
Lloyd and Jennifer Laing, Thames and Hudson, 1992

More information and examples of the art of Courtney Davis can be found at:
www.celtic-art.com

Dennis O'Neill is of Irish ancestry and was born and brought up in Chicago, where he is now a Roman Catholic priest. He is a Celtic specialist, and has contributed to a number of books on Celtic history and culture.